W9-BHU-332

FIRST MATH

By
Joanna Brundle

Published in 2018 by
KidHaven Publishing, an Imprint of Greenhaven Publishing, LLC
353 3rd Avenue
Suite 255
New York, NY 10010

Designer: Danielle Jones
Editor: Joanna Brundle

Cataloging-in-Publication Data

Names: Brundle, Joanna.
Title: Shapes / Joanna Brundle.
Description: New York : KidHaven Publishing, 2018. | Series: First math | Includes index.
Identifiers: ISBN 9781534522077 (pbk.) | ISBN 9781534521902 (library bound) | ISBN 9781534521827 (6 pack) | ISBN 9781534521865 (ebook)
Subjects: LCSH: Shapes–Juvenile literature. | Geometry–Juvenile literature.
Classification: LCC QA445.5 B78 2018 | DDC 516.15–dc23

Printed in the United States of America

CPSIA compliance information: Batch #BS17KL: For further information contact Greenhaven Publishing LLC, New York, New York at 1-844-317-7404.

Please visit our website, www.greenhavenpublishing.com. For a free color catalog of all our
high-quality books, call toll free 1-844-317-7404 or fax 1-844-317-7405.

PHOTO CREDITS

**Abbreviations: l-left, r-right, b-bottom,
t-top, c-center, m-middle.**

Front cover – Gladskikh Tatiana. 3 – Bloomua. 5 – Robert Anthony. 6 – ideldesign. 7 – Dmitry Naumov. 9 – Nicolesa. 10 – izzzy71. 11 – omphoto. 13 – Di Studio. 14 – ChameleonsEye.
15 – SOMMAI. 17 – witittorn onkhaw. 18 – ADfoto. 22 – Peter Vrabel. 23 – MAGRIT HIRSCH.

Images are courtesy of Shutterstock.com, with thanks to Getty Images, Thinkstock Photo, and iStockphoto.

CONTENTS

Trace the shapes with your finger as you read.

SQUARES

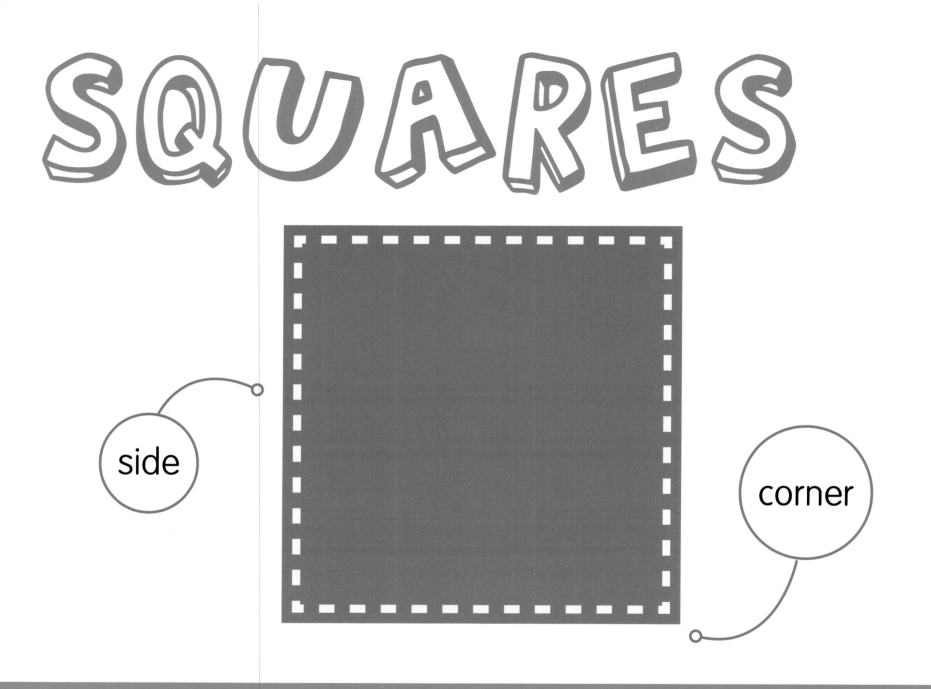

side

corner

A square has four sides and four corners.

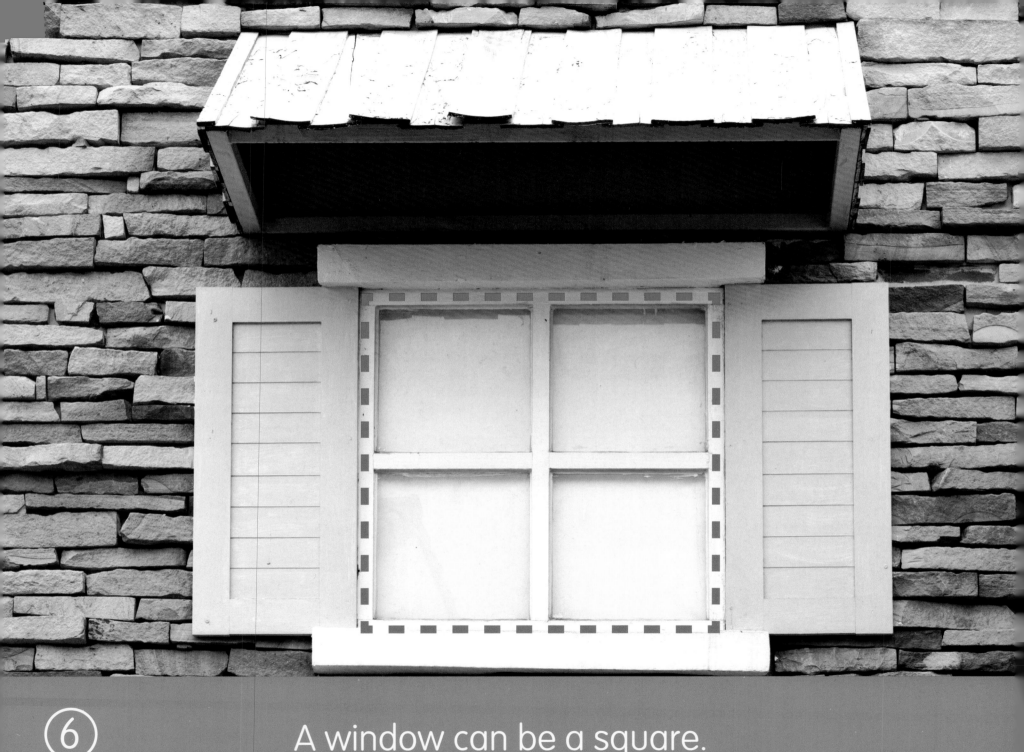

⑥ A window can be a square.

Tiles can be squares.

RECTANGLES

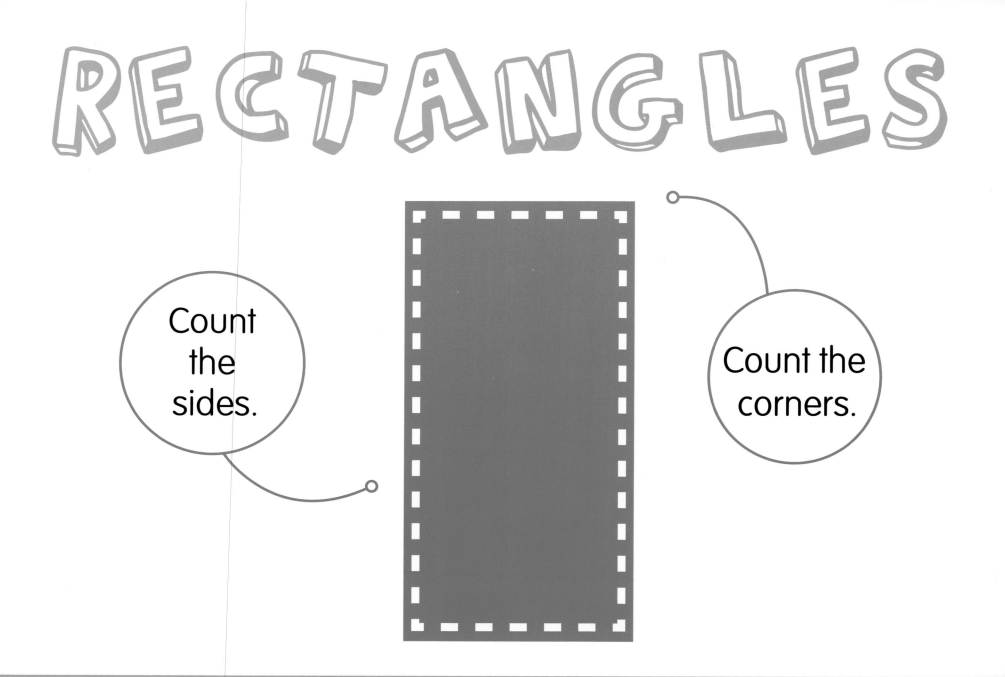

Count the sides.

Count the corners.

A rectangle has four sides and four corners.

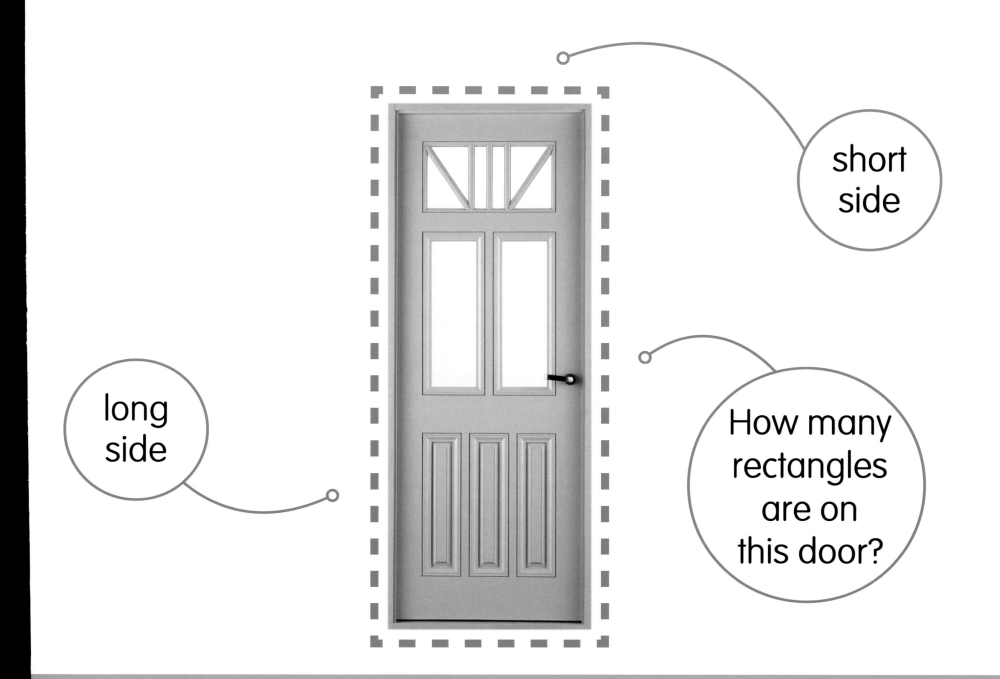

short side

long side

How many rectangles are on this door?

A rectangle has two short sides and two long sides. ⑨

Happy Birthday!

A birthday card can be a rectangle.

A chocolate bar can be a rectangle.

CIRCLES

curved

A circle is round. It is a closed, curved shaped.

A circle has no sides and no corners.

 You can see circles on a tree stump.

Cucumber slices look like circles.

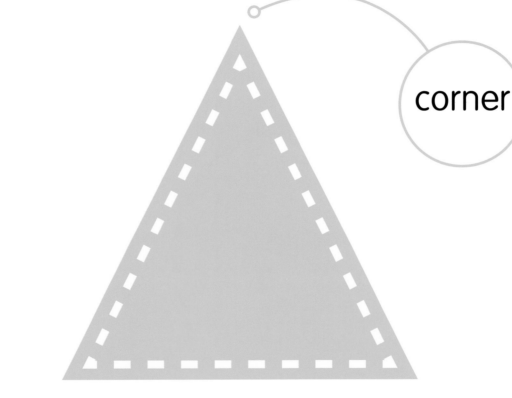

corner

 A triangle has three sides and three corners.

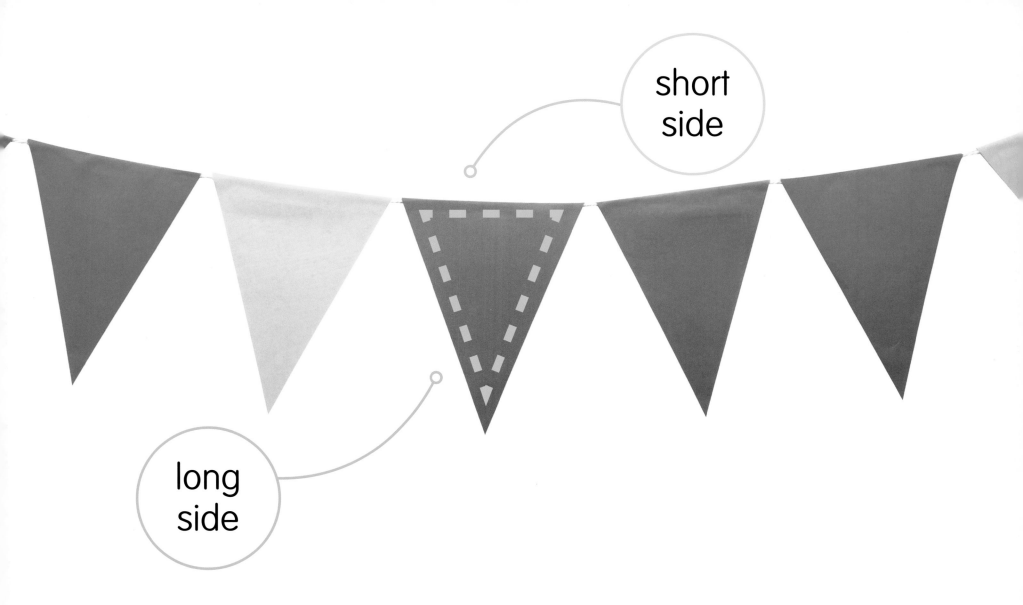

short
side

long
side

The sides can be the same size or different sizes.

18 A pizza slice can be a triangle.

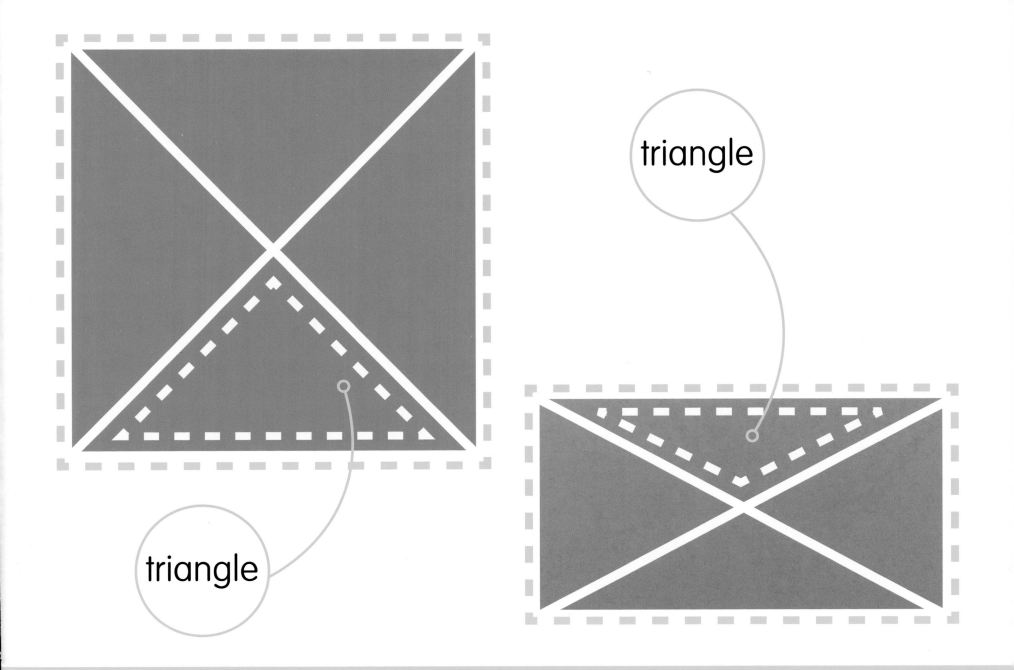

triangle

triangle

Four triangles can make a square or a rectangle.

OTHER SHAPES

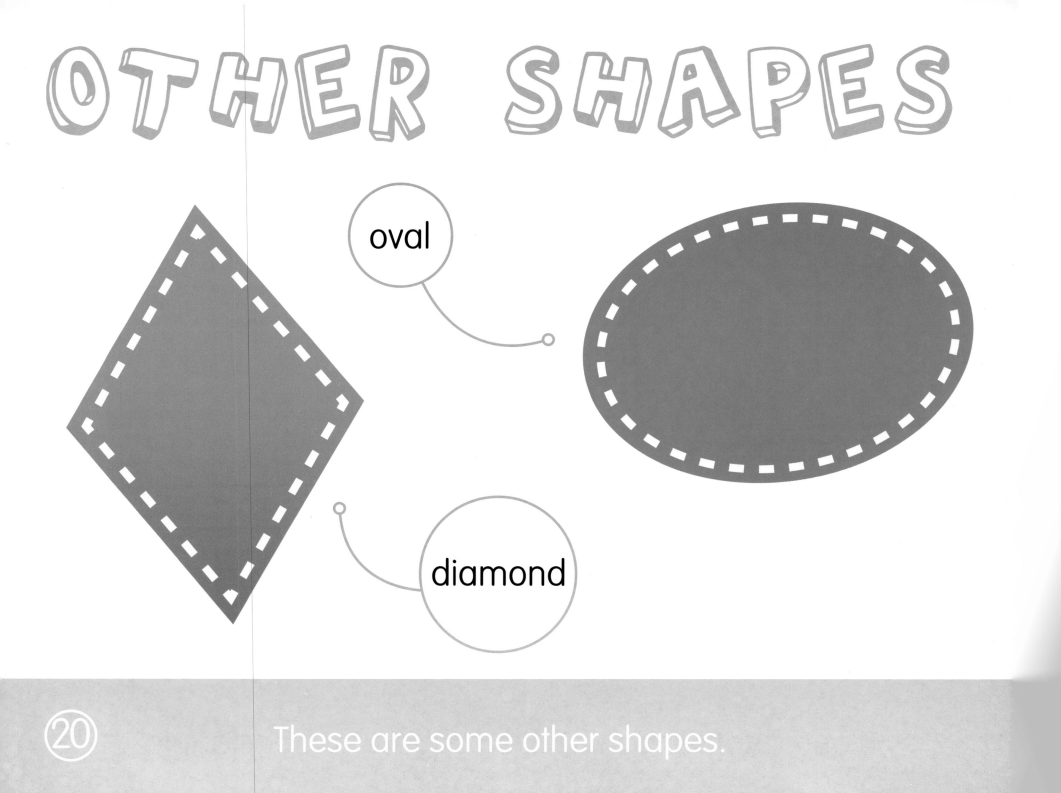

oval

diamond

These are some other shapes.

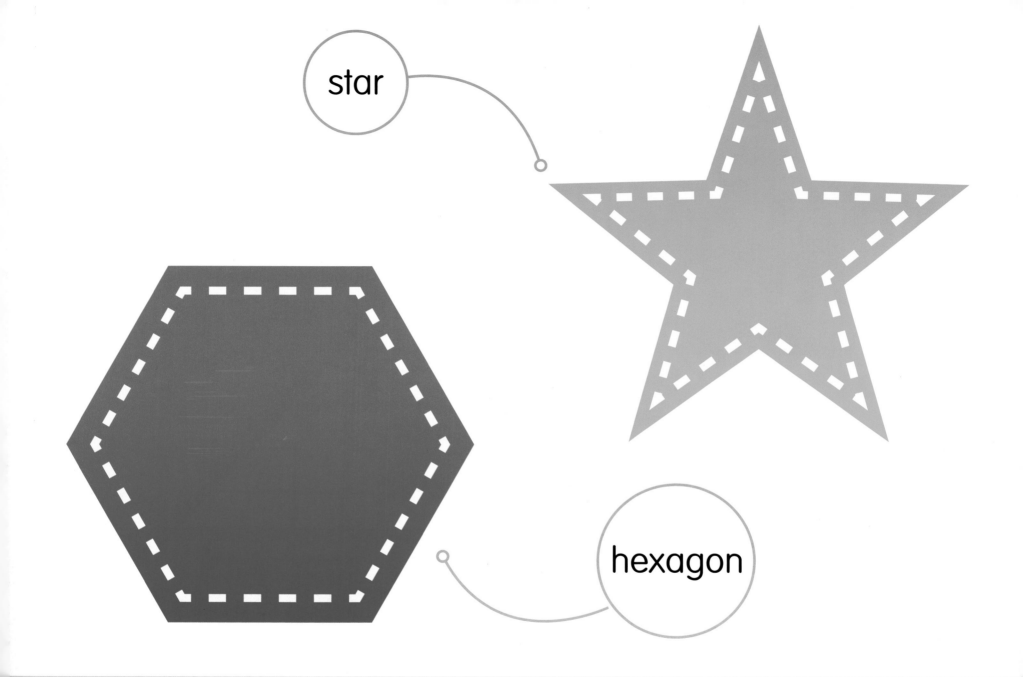

star

hexagon

WHAT SHAPES CAN YOU SEE?

 What shapes can you see on this house?

Drop a stone in a puddle. What shapes do you see? The answers to these questions are on page 24.

What shapes can you see on this quilt?

ANSWERS

HOUSE: triangles, rectangles, squares

QUILT: rectangles, squares, triangles, diamonds, ovals

A stone dropped in a puddle makes circles.